History of America

SPANISH MISSIONS

Forever Changing the People of the Old West

Written by **Nadia Higgins**

Rourke
Educational Media

rourkeeducationalmedia.com

www.rourkeeducationalmedia.com

PHOTO CREDITS: Library of Congress, cover (lower right), 2, 7, 15, 19, 28, 37 top, 38, 39, 40, 45 bottom, 46 (top first column, fourth first column, last first column, top second column, third second column, last second column); iStockphoto, 4, 5, 10, 12, 16, 17 (background), 20, 21, 22, 25, 29, 30, 31, 32, 34, 41, 43, 46 (fourth last column); Stock Montage, cover (upper right), 37; North Wind Picture Archives, cover (upper left), 9, 24; John Sandford, 27, 33, 44 (top), 46 (second and third first column); Chalk Butte, Inc., 45; Phil Martin Photography, cover (lower left), 6, 14, 17 (forefront), 26, 35, 42

Edited by Jill Sherman

Cover design by Nicola Stratford, bdpublishing.com

Interior layout by Jen Thomas

Library of Congress PCN Data

Higgins, Nadia
Spanish Missions: Forever Changing the People of the Old West / Nadia Higgins
 ISBN 978-1-62169-833-3 (hard cover)
 ISBN 978-1-62169-728-2 (soft cover)
 ISBN 978-1-62169-937-8 (e-Book)
Library of Congress Control Number: 2013936381

Also Available as:

ROURKE'S
e-Books

Rourke Educational Media
Printed in the United States of America,
North Mankato, Minnesota

Rourke
Educational Media

rourkeeducationalmedia.com

customerservice@rourkeeducationalmedia.com • PO Box 643328 Vero Beach, Florida 32964

Table of Contents

Chapter I
Daily Duties at the Mission

The bells rang out as the first streaks of sunlight appeared on the horizon. This was the sound that began the day at a California mission.

In the early nineteenth century, most of present-day California was wild and rugged land. The Spanish mission was a walled-in town rising out of the desert. As the day wore on and the sun climbed higher in the sky, the walls of the mission turned golden brown. They were made of **adobe**, bricks molded from mud and straw. Several feet thick, these adobe walls helped control who could enter and exit the mission.

Bells and cross of the Mission San Miguel, California

Jutting above the walls was an impressive stone church. The church was far more beautiful than the other buildings. In the slanted morning light, the wooden cross on top of the building cast a long shadow. The cross announced the mission's purpose, to spread Christianity throughout the region.

Different buildings served other important aspects of the mission. Buildings for making leather, cloth, soap, and candles, for forging metal, and for preparing food would soon be buzzing with the sounds of workers. Outside the mission walls, fields of wheat, barley, and other crops were ready to be tended. Farther out, hundreds, sometimes thousands, of cattle grazed on the land.

Three main groups of people lived in the mission: hundreds of Native Americans, two or three **Catholic** priests, or padres as they were called, and six or so Spanish soldiers. The Native Americans were the reason for the mission. The padres wanted them to give up their religion and culture. As much as possible, they were to become Christians with European ways and manners. The Native Americans were also the mission's workers.

The sound of the bell called the Native Americans to morning prayers. They headed from their cramped quarters to the church. After prayers was a full day of work, meals, more prayers, and religious instruction. Each event in their daily schedule would be announced by tolling bells.

A CHILD'S LIFE AT A MISSION

Children played a special role in mission life. In the eyes of the padres, children represented the future success of the missions. Unlike their parents, they easily picked up the Spanish language and customs.

At some missions, the padres tried to keep parents from teaching Native American ways to their children. The children were forced to live in separate buildings from their adult relatives.

Children spent much of the day at church and learning the Spanish language and crafts. Girls were taught to weave, sew, cook, and make pottery. Boys learned skills such as preparing leather from cowhide, blacksmithing, carpentry, and painting.

Children were also made to work. They could chase hungry birds away from the crops. They helped pick vegetables and fruits. A boy might also assist in the ringing of the bells. At Mission San Juan Capistrano in California, boys helped turn the stone mill that crushed olives for making oil. Older boys stomped on grapes with their bare feet to make wine.

A magazine illustration from 1877 shows Native Americans on a California mission weaving baskets and rope.

"There yet remains the ruins of an immense church, which was destroyed by an earthquake in 1812, when many Native Americans were buried in its fall. It still bears the appearance of having been one of the best finished structures in the country."

Alfred Robinson, a New England trader who visited California in the 1830s and 1840s, describing the San Juan Capistrano Mission in his book Life in California

Two or three Spanish padres had the job of running things in the day ahead. They were the teachers and the rule makers of the mission community. They saw themselves as the shepherds of the **natives**' souls.

One of the priests had woken in darkness in his simply furnished room. He had put on his **habit**, a coarse gray robe with a rope belt, and gone to ring the bell that started the day.

In the barracks, the soldiers were roused to duty. The men put on their uniforms. They wore thick leather vests to protect them from arrows. They gathered their swords and long rifles. The soldiers were in charge of maintaining order at the mission. One of their main duties was making sure none of the Native Americans ran away, and chasing down and whipping those who did.

> "I scarcely know what to do in these troublesome times. I made the vows of a priest; instead I must manage temporalities, sow grain, raise sheep, horses and cows. I must preach, baptize, bury the dead, visit the sick, direct the carts, haul stones…"
>
> *A padre at Mission San Juan Bautista, California, in a letter to a New Spanish government official*

It was the start of a typical day during the height of the California missions. But dozens of other missions in what is now the American Southwest had already come and gone. Even prosperous California missions such as this one would fall into ruins in just a few decades.

From around 1600 to the 1830s, mission communities dotted the landscape of present-day New Mexico, Texas, Arizona, and California. These areas were not yet part of the United States. Instead, first Spain and, after 1821, Mexico ruled the land. The missions were an attempt by Spanish rulers to turn Native Amercans into loyal Spanish subjects. The attempt failed, but missions forever changed the people of the American Southwest.

As priests exit a mission chapel, Native Americans stop their activities and kneel to show respect.

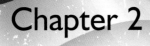

Chapter 2

Unrealistic Expectations

Traditionally, the founding of the United States has been a story about the East Coast. In 1620, the Pilgrims arrived at Plymouth Rock, Massachusetts. English settlers came to the New World and forced Native Americans from their lands. They founded 13 **colonies**, which later became America's first 13 states.

Mission Santa Barbara, California

But what was happening in the West at that time? That is another story of Europeans coming to the New World. These Europeans came from Spain instead of England and their purpose was often different. Few Spaniards came to live on the land themselves. Instead, Spanish priests led expeditions into the wilderness. Instead of colonies, they set up missions. Instead of settlers, Native Americans populated the missions. In every way possible, the priests tried to make the Native Americans resemble Spaniards.

When missionaries arrived in California in 1769, about 100,000 Native Americans lived in the area. They belonged to 60 different tribes speaking 90 different languages. By 1823, 21,750 Native Americans were living on 21 missions. The Native Americans outnumbered Spanish settlers and soldiers by about six to one.

Why did they do it? The answer is twofold: On the one hand, they came on the urging of the government of Spain. During the seventeenth and eighteenth centuries, the countries of Europe competed for land in North America. Spain had controlled a vast area they called New Spain since the early sixteenth century. New Spain stretched from what is now Mexico to the American Southwest.

An old map showing North America, including what is now Mexico and the United States, in the seventeenth century.

The heart of New Spain was in present-day Mexico, where the Spanish hold on the territory was strong. Here, Spaniards had conquered huge Native American populations and controlled the largest cities and most valuable mines in the New World. However, the king of Spain was worried about the lands just north of Mexico. Although his country had claimed the area, few Spaniards had settled there. The dry, desert land held little promise for colonists. And the journey from Mexico was difficult.

Furthermore, Spain simply did not have enough citizens to occupy all the land it had claimed. Without Spanish towns there, Spain's hold on the northern frontier was weak. What was to stop France, England, or even Russia from claiming this land for itself?

ONE NATIVE AMERICAN'S STORY

Today, restored missions are some of the most beautiful historical sites in California and the American Southwest. The candlelit churches and lush gardens give the impression of a lovely, romantic past. In reality, mission life was often harsh and marked by violence. Today, most Native Americans look back on the mission period as a sad chapter in their tribal history.

Following is an actual account of a Native American's mission experience, told when he was an old man, in 1878. His name was Janitin, and he was a Kamia of southern California.

"When we arrived at the mission, they locked me in a room for a week; the father … told me many things that I did not understand. … The following day … they took me to work with the other Indians. … In the afternoon they lashed me for not finishing the job, and the following day the same thing. … One day I found a way to escape, but I was tracked and they caught me … they seized me by lasso as on the first occasion, and they carried me off to the mission. … After we arrived, the father … ordered that they fasten me to the stake. They lashed me until I lost consciousness."

Missions promised a solution to this problem. Though few Spanish settlers lived in the territory, tens of thousands, perhaps even a million or more, of Native Americans did. Native Americans had been living in the area for more than 10,000 years. Why not **convert** the natives into Spanish-speaking, Spanish-thinking, Spanish-acting residents? Then they would protect the land from invading countries.

So the padres were sent to the Old West to set up missions to protect Spain's interests. However, they also had a second, personal reason. The padres felt it was their responsibility to make Native Americans give up their own religions and become Christians. The priests were Catholic, and they truly believed that anybody who died without believing in Christ would go

> Priests kept careful records of what went on at the missions. They kept track of data such as the number of Native American converts and the results of yearly harvests. The Native Americans, on the other hand, usually didn't have a written language and no way to keep such records, which means that most of what we know of mission life is told from the padres' point of view.

to eternal damnation, or what some call hell. Looking back, one might think the priests were self-centered in believing that only their religion held any value. Still, in their eyes, they were providing the Native Americans with eternal happiness, at least after death.

The original idea behind the missions was that they would be temporary. The padres and the Spanish authorities thought it would take about 10 years to train the Native Americans to live in villages as productive, Christian, Spanish persons. When that was accomplished, the fathers were to give the missions over to Native American control.

This never happened. Many missions operated for 50 or 60 years. In the 1830s, those missions that hadn't failed on their own were taken over by the Mexican government. The land was broken up and sold or given to farmers and ranchers. Most Native Americans went to work for the new owners.

The only surviving original adobe mission building, a dormitory for Native American residents, has been restored as part of the Santa Cruz Mission State Historic Park as the Neary-Rodriguez Adobe.

Chapter 3

First Missions

The site of the first mission in the Old West is marked by a sign posted by the New Mexico Highway Department. Thirty miles (48 kilometers) north of Santa Fe, New Mexico, the sign commemorates the founding of Mission San Juan de los Caballeros in 1598.

Completed in 1816, the San Francisco de Assisi Mission Church with massive adobe buttresses and two front-facing bell towers, remains an important center of community life to the citizens of Ranchos de Taos.

The story of the mission begins in Mexico with a Spanish adventurer named Juan de Oñate. Oñate was not a priest but a miner. He traveled north in search of gold, silver, and other riches. Behind him, a line of 84 wagons snaked for miles across the desert. Accompanying Oñate were about 500 settlers and their servants, 7,000 farm animals, loads of tools, seeds, and food, and 10 padres. Oñate himself would return to Mexico empty-handed, but many of the settlers stayed, as did the missionaries. In the following decades, the priests oversaw the construction of dozens of missions in New Mexico.

Oñate crossed the Rio Grande and with a long, flowery speech, claimed New Mexico for Spain. Then he marched up the river with a select crew of men, including the priests. Oñate and his men traveled almost 400 miles (640 kilometers) until they set up headquarters at a Native American pueblo, or town, called Okhay. The Spaniards drove the natives out of their houses, then moved into the empty dwellings themselves. They renamed the pueblo San Juan de los Caballeros, which became the site of the church marked by the highway sign today.

While traveling through what is now the New Mexican desert, Oñate believed he discovered a passage to the Gulf of California. He recorded the event by carving a message, in Spanish, on a rock.

Oñate then divided New Mexico into seven districts and assigned the areas to the 10 priests. That meant that one or two men were to go out alone into the vast, unknown land to build missions.

> "I find myself today with my full and entire camp near the river which they call Del Norte, and on the bank which is contiguous to the first towns of New Mexico, and whereas I wish to take possession of the land today, the day of the Ascension of our Lord, dated April 30th, of the present year 1598."
>
> *Juan de Oñate, in his speech taking possession of New Mexico for Spain, as recorded by the king's clerk, Juan Pérez de Donís*

The priests faced enormous challenges. They set out to convert Native Americans, but the two groups didn't speak the same language. The priests were to convince the Native Americans to accept Christianity, but the Native Americans already had their own religions. Their religions were based on nature and involved praying to many gods. To them, the idea of worshipping just one god was strange. Furthermore, the Spaniards had no specific training in construction, yet they were given the task of designing and building churches. They had carried only the most essential tools with them and little or no building materials. They would have to rely almost entirely on the Native Americans to find materials and perform the labor.

But would the Native Americans cooperate with them? Oñate's 10 priests were not the first to try to establish missions in New Mexico. Stories of padres killed by **hostile** natives were familiar among the Spaniards.

Nevertheless, the priests carried on. Believing they were doing God's work, they saw no obstacle as an excuse to back down.

Though the history of missions in New Spain is full of failed attempts, dozens of missions were successful, at least for a time, and some even thrived. For most Native Americans in the Old West, joining a mission meant leaving one's home, giving up one's religion, speaking a new language, and working without pay. What made them do it?

"Oñate told them that he had been sent by the most powerful king and ruler in the world, Don Philip, king of Spain, who desired especially to serve God our Lord and to bring about the salvation of their souls, but wished also to have them as his subjects and to protect and bring justice to them."

Juan Pérez de Donís, King Philip's clerk, in a report describing a meeting between Oñate and Native American leaders, 1598

ADOBE

Often priests arrived in the deserts of the Southwest with a handful of tools and little or no building materials. So, like the Native Americans, they turned to materials that could be found all around them, like sand, clay, and straw. For hundreds of years, Native American women of New Mexico had been constructing their family homes from adobe, a mixture of these three ingredients. Layer by layer, Native American women stacked and molded the mud into walls. The Spanish priests introduced the idea of making bricks out of the adobe. Adobe brick became the main building block of most missions in North America.

Most mission buildings were made of a mixture of sand, clay, and straw called adobe.

To make adobe bricks, a thick mud mixture was packed into a rectangular wooden mold that looked like a box with no bottom. When the mud was hard enough but still damp, the mold was lifted away. Now the mold could be used to form more bricks. The damp block of mud was left in the sun to dry for another four or five weeks before it was ready for use.

Each adobe brick weighed about 50 pounds (22.7 kilograms) and was about six times the size of a familiar red brick. Adobe bricks were quite strong but required a lot of repair as wind, heat, and rain wore away the dried mud.

Once padres arrived at a good site for a mission, they would start by trying to befriend the Native Americans. Because the priests didn't speak the natives' language, they tried ringing bells and playing music. Sometimes the Native Americans would approach out of curiosity and, once there, stay to receive gifts such as glass beads and ribbons. The priests tried to persuade the Native American leader to join, because that was often a shortcut to getting the whole tribe to come out. Some Native Americans came because they were sick, or their children were sick, and they believed the padres had good medicine. Others joined because they saw the mission as a way to protect themselves from their enemies. Sometimes Native Americans

> "By using certain herbs, roots, and feathers and other items, Native Americans believe they can free themselves from their enemies and from illnesses."
>
> *Fathers Catalá and Viader, 1814 report from Mission Santa Clara*

were captured and then forced to stay. One strategy was for soldiers to capture the women and children of a tribe and thus force the men to follow their families.

Even when Native Americans willingly joined, most did not realize they would have to live at the missions for the rest of their lives. Native Americans resisted mission life in a number of ways. They practiced their own traditions or mixed them in with the Catholic **rituals**. Some tried to escape. Some organized uprisings that brought down dozens of missions in New Spain's northern frontier.

Chapter 4
New Mexico Missions

The story of Spanish missions is depicted in the buildings themselves. The very first mission buildings were the biggest. The enthusiastic priests who oversaw their

A mission in Golden, New Mexico

construction expected to fill the large missions with great numbers of converted Native Americans. As time went on, and missionaries began to face the realities of their task, the buildings got smaller and smaller.

San Miguel Mission is a Spanish colonial mission church in Santa Fe, New Mexico. Built between 1610 and 1626, it is claimed to be the oldest church in the United States.

Pueblo people lived in adobe houses known as pueblos, which are multi-story house complexes made of adobe and stone. Each adobe unit was home to one family, like a modern day apartment.

While the success of missions in the Old West varied enormously, almost all of them faced incredible hardships at one time or another. In addition to floods, earthquakes, and **drought**, missions were often attacked by hostile natives. Mission residents were often hungry. Most damaging were the diseases that spread wildly through the crowded Native American quarters. The Spaniards had unknowingly brought diseases such as smallpox and measles to the Americas. Because the diseases were common in Europe, the Spaniards' had built up a resistance to them. Once introduced to the Native American populations these illnesses proved devastating. In California, the number of Native Americans fell by two-thirds between the founding of the first mission in 1769 and the end of missions in the 1830s.

Missionaries in New Mexico had an advantage over those who would later work in other areas. Many Native American tribes were nomadic hunters and gatherers. They didn't live in permanent villages but moved around depending on where wild plants and animals were plentiful. The New Mexico Native Americans lived in towns, called pueblos, and farmed for a living. The missionaries and the Pueblos, as they came to be called, shared farming techniques with each other. Also, because the Pueblos already lived in villages, the priests didn't have to find and move them to the missionary site. They simply built missions near existing pueblos.

Popé (1630-1688)

Between 1598 and 1680, about 50 missions were established throughout New Mexico. By 1680 trouble had developed between the Pueblos and the Spaniards. The priests had strict rules against allowing the Native Americans to practice their own religions. And the rules were sometimes violently enforced by Spanish soldiers.

In 1680, the Pueblo leader Popé led a bloody uprising against the Spaniards in New Mexico. Some historians have called it the most successful Native American uprising in the American West. The Native Americans killed 21 missionaries and 400 Spanish settlers. Then they chased almost all the other Spaniards out of New Mexico. The only remaining Europeans were wives of Native American men.

The group of fleeing Spaniards resettled in what is now El Paso, Texas. Twelve years later they returned to New Mexico. Within that time Popé had died and many Pueblos accepted the padres return.

Chapter 5

The Missions of Arizona and Texas

The first mission in Texas, Corpus Christi de la Isleta, was established in 1682 for the Native Americans who had fled from New Mexico with the Spaniards. But Texas missions began in earnest two years later when French ships landed on the eastern coast of Texas. The alarmed Spanish government moved to secure its hold on the region by building a group of missions there.

Mission San Xavier del Bac, Arizona

Concepción Mission in San Antonio, Texas was built in 1731.

At first, these missions weren't as successful as the ones in New Mexico. Unlike the Pueblos, the Native Americans here were nomadic, and resistant to settling in one place. And there was still the problem of European diseases wiping out entire communities.

Then, Father Antonio Olivares came up with a plan. The Spaniards would build new, more effective missions in the San Antonio area and close the failing missions of eastern Texas.

The Alamo was built in 1718.

The Alamo mission has been restored into one of Texas's most popular tourist attractions. More than 2.5 million people visit the Alamo each year.

Olivares oversaw the founding of a cluster of missions around San Antonio that today make up some of the state's most visited historical sites. One of these, San Antonio de Valero, would come to play an important role in the history of the United States. The mission is better known as the Alamo, a nickname Spanish soldiers gave it describing nearby cottonwood trees. In 1836, more than 40 years after the Alamo had stopped operating as a mission, Texans used it as a fort in a bloody battle with Mexican troops. The episode eventually led to the American takeover of the region.

The story of Arizona missions is quite different from that of others in the region. These few missions were largely the work of one priest, Eusebio Francisco Kino. Kino worked with the Pima tribe of northern Mexico and Arizona from 1687 until 1711 and founded more than 24 missions in the area.

Today a statue of Father Eusebio Francisco Kino represents the state of Arizona in the U.S. Capitol in Washington, D.C.

The entrance to an old mission chapel in San Antonio, Texas.

Though Kino reported to the Spanish government, he was Italian. As a young man, Kino became very sick and almost died. He made a vow that when he got better, he would become a priest.

DESERT FARMS

At missions, wild desert had to be turned into farmland to support the crops needed for survival. How did the Spaniards make the dry soil suitable for growing wheat, barley, corn, and other crops? They built systems of ditches, dams, and channels called aqueducts. These **irrigation** systems carried water from nearby sources to the desert land. In Arizona, the padres followed Native Americans who had been using irrigation for more than 1,000 years.

Near the old Mission San Francisco de la Espada in Texas, there remains a little bit of what was once a complex irrigation project. Between 1731 and 1745 the Native Americans, under the supervision of the missionaries, dug a 15-mile (24-kilometer) system of ditches. With the help of five dams and an aqueduct, this system took water from the San Antonio River and irrigated 3,500 acres (1,400 hectares) of land. The system was powered only by the force of gravity. The water channels had to be angled properly so that the water would flow downhill. The main ditch continues to carry water to the mission and its former farmlands even today.

Kino is remembered as a peacemaker. He didn't believe in forcing Native Americans to accept Christianity. At his missions, the Native Americans came and went freely. Kino hoped to make

Eusebio Francisco Kino (1645-1711)

Christianity attractive to the Native Americans through his own example.

"There are already … abundant fields … of wheat, maize, frijoles, chickpeas, beans, lentils. … There are orchards, and in them vineyards for wine for the Masses. … There are many Castilian fruit trees, such as figs, quinces, oranges, pomegranates, peaches, apricots, pears, apples, mulberries, etc."

Eusebio Francisco Kino,
describing an Arizona mission, 1710

Spanish officials did not always approve of Kino's methods. At one point, another priest was sent to the area to determine whether or not Kino's missions should be shut down. When the priest discovered the peaceful, productive mission communities, Kino was allowed to continue his life's work.

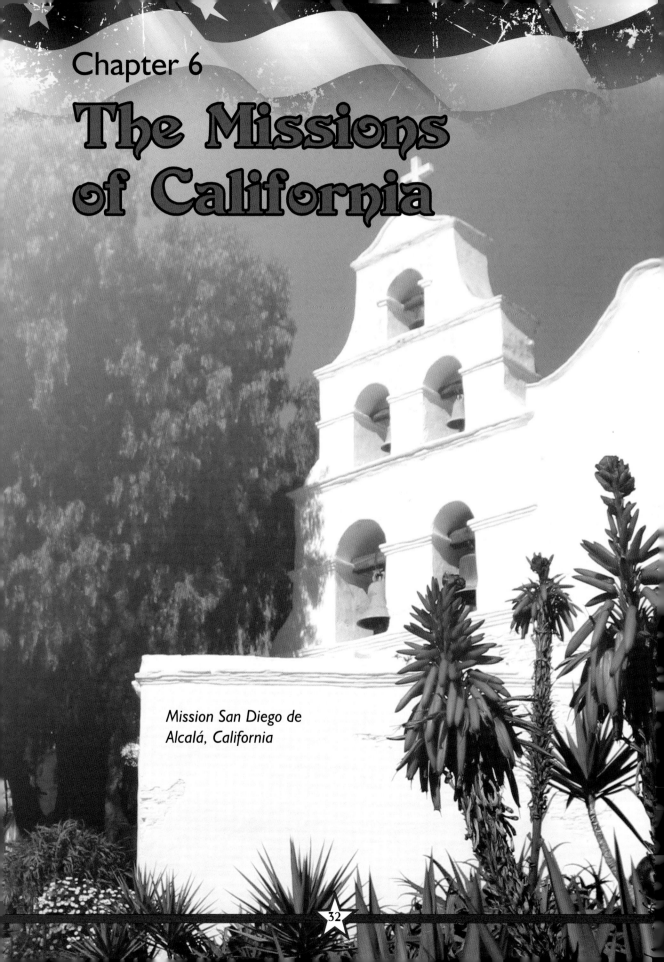

Chapter 6
The Missions of California

Mission San Diego de Alcalá, California

Like those in New Mexico and Texas, the missions founded by Kino had fallen on hard times by the second half of the eighteenth century. Natural disasters, disease, and Native American uprisings led to the decline of the missions.

It is not surprising, then, that Spain was not eager to start a new chain of missions in California in the 1760s. California was the most remote frontier of New Spain, and crossing from Mexico meant having to confront imposing mountains and hostile Native Americans.

"I do not know what security His Majesty can have in his conscience for delaying so long to send ministers of the Gospel to this realm of California."

Father Ascensión, 1620

A book of Bible readings from the eighteenth century.

But when Russian fur traders, who had already established themselves in Alaska, headed for California, the king of Spain became alarmed. Would Russia try to take over the land? He sent a group of soldiers, settlers, and priests north from Mexico to secure Spain's claim on California.

CATTLE PARTS

Cattle were especially valuable on California missions. The animals were used for much more than just food. Cowhides were called California bank notes, because they were used like money to pay for items that couldn't be produced at the missions, such as silk, chocolate, and tea.

At the mission, Native American men processed cowhides into leather at the tannery. The leather was used for saddles, boots, and rope. Nails were in short supply, so strips of leather held together the wooden beams of many mission roofs. Priests' beds were wooden frames with leather straps stretched across them. Thin, opaque hides were even used to cover windows. Tannery workers shaved the hair off the cowhide, then rubbed it with oil until it shone almost like glass.

Tallow, hard fat that was scraped from cowhides, was used to make soap and candles. Native American women made candles by dipping long strings, or wicks, into melted tallow dozens of times. The tallow cooled into thick layers of fat around the wick. For soap, tallow was boiled with a flaky, white chemical called lye. The mixture cooled and hardened and then was cut into bars.

Father Junípero Serra walked much of the 700-mile (1,127-kilometer) trip. During the 93-day journey, about half of his party either died or gave up. Serra arrived in San Diego exhausted but not discouraged. Sixteen days later, he began work on the first mission in California, San Diego de Alcalá. This first California mission was a simple log building plastered together with mud.

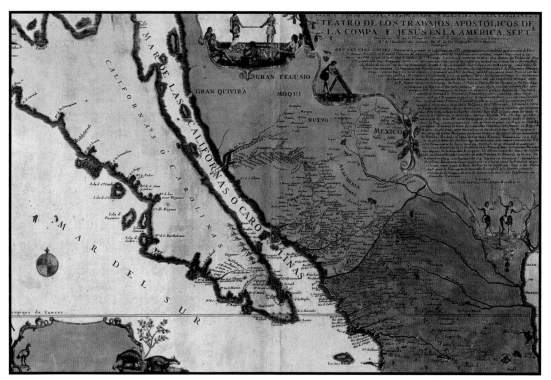

A 1720 map of California and Mexico shows California, in yellow, as an island.

"Then we all made our way to a gigantic cross which was all in readiness and lying on the ground. With everyone lending a hand we set it in an upright position. … After raising aloft the cross, we unfurled the flag of our Catholic Monarch likewise. As we raised each one of them, we shouted at the top of our voices: 'Long live the Faith! Long live the King!'"

Father Junípero Serra's account of the founding of California's first mission, San Diego de Alcalá

Founded in 1769, Mission San Diego de Alcalá was California's first church.

Within the next 50 years, some of the region's most prosperous missions would line the coast of California. After San Diego, Serra himself oversaw the construction of eight more missions. Then his successor, Padre Fermín Francisco de Lasuén, built nine more. In the end, 21 missions stretched in a chain from San Diego to San Francisco.

Father Junípero Serra's bedroom at a California mission.

> "If placed at proper intervals … they would form from San Diego to here Mission San Carlos, in Carmel, stepping stones, so that every third day one might sleep in a village. With that, peace would be assured, and passage through all the country made easy; and a postal service may be established."
>
> **Father Junípero Serra in a letter to a Mexican official, August 24, 1774**

A 1787 drawing of Father Junípero Serra shows him preaching to a crowd of Native Americans.

Each mission was a one- to three-day's walk from the next. The dirt path that connected them was called the Camino Real, or Royal Road. Today, California's well-known Highway 101 basically follows the route of the Camino Real.

Chapter 7

From Missions to Memories

By the 1820s, missions were thriving in California. Many were huge centers of manufactured goods, such as leather, soap, candles, and blankets. Their farmlands and ranches stretched for miles outside the mission walls.

At the same time, however, Spain's presence in the American Southwest was coming to an end. In 1821, Mexican rebels overthrew Spanish rule and started an independent nation. The struggling new country had neither the desire nor the funds to continue the missionary system. By 1834, the Mexican government had taken over the missions. The priests left the churches, and the land was divided and sold.

A National Historic Landmark, San Xavier Mission in Arizona is constructed of low-fire clay brick and stone and lime mortor. The entire structure is roofed with masonary vaults, making it unique among Spanish Colonial buildings.

Many Native Americans had no choice but to stay on to work for the farmers and ranchers who bought the land. Others looked for work in nearby towns. Some were able to return to their tribes. However, life was never the same for them.

Even the land itself was forever changed. The Spaniards had brought the first cattle to the West. They had introduced plants such as orange trees and crops such as wheat and barely. Native Americans had lived off nature by fishing, hunting, and gathering wild nuts and berries. That way of life was becoming more and more difficult.

Today people light candles as a form of prayer at the Mission San Luis Rey in southern California.

Without anybody taking care of them, most of the mission buildings fell into disrepair. The wooden roof timbers rotted, then collapsed. With no protection from the rain and wind, the adobe walls were the next to go.

Toward the end of the nineteenth century and especially in the early twentieth century, people became interested in restoring the missions. Scholars retrieved old records and diaries and tried to rebuild the missions just as they had been. When visiting a mission, keep in mind that it may have been restored or, in some cases, completely rebuilt.

Today, many missions are working Catholic parishes. The old churches were reopened to serve the descendants of the Native Americans, soldiers, and Spanish settlers who had lived on the land in those early days.

A restored Mission San Inés, the 19th of California's 21 missions, is an active parish today.

Biographies

Many people played important roles throughout this time period. Learn more about them in the Biographies section.

Oñate, Juan de (1550-1626) - A Spanish explorer born in Zacatecas, Mexico, Oñate left for New Mexico in search of riches in 1598. Although he did not find riches, he is remembered for colonizing the area for New Spain. Oñate served as governor of the New Mexican colonies until 1607, when he was forced to step down by settlers who accused him of abusing his power.

Popé (1630-1688) - Popé was a Native American from present-day New Mexico. In the 1670s he became angry with the Spanish priests for the way they treated Native Americans, in particular, for forbidding them to practice their own religion. Popé began organizing a revolt with other Native Americans in the area, and in August of 1680 he and his warriors waged a full-scale rebellion. Under Popé's skillful planning and leadership, the Native Americans succeeded in driving away the Spanish for many years. They killed 21 priests and more than 400 colonists.

Olivares, Antonio (1630-1722) - Olivares was a Spanish missionary who, in the early 1700s, came up with a plan for saving Texas missions. In 1718, Olivares founded the San Antonio de Valero mission, better known as the Alamo, in present-day San Antonio. In 1836, the Alamo was used as a fort in a key battle between Texans and Mexican troops during the Texas Revolution. The restored mission is one of the state's most visited tourist sites.

Kino, Eusebio Francisco (1645-1711) - Kino was an Italian priest who was sent by the Spanish government to establish missions in present-day Arizona and northern Mexico. He founded at least 24 missions in the area. Kino was also an explorer and mapmaker. One of his maps showed that California was not an island, as most Europeans had previously thought. Kino is remembered as a peacemaker between warring Native American tribes and also between the Spaniards and the Native Americans. A statue of Kino represents Arizona in the U.S. Capitol in Washington, D.C.

Serra, Junípero (1713-1784) - Serra was born to peasant farmers in Mallorca, Spain. At the age of 36, considered to be quite old in his day, he decided to give up the comfortable life of a university professor to become a missionary in New Spain. Serra was neither big nor strong, but he overcame many hardships and eventually established nine missions in California. The Catholic Church is considering making him a saint.

Lasuén, Fermín Francisco de (1736-1803) - Born in Spain, Lasuén traveled to Mexico at the age of 25 to work as a missionary in New Spain. In addition to founding nine missions in California, he continued work on many of those started by Junípero Serra.

Timeline

1521
Spanish explorer Hernán Cortés conquers parts of present-day Mexico, establishing New Spain.

Around 1600
The first mission in the Old West is established in New Mexico.

1680
Pueblo leader Popé leads a successful revolt against Spaniards in New Mexico.

1691
Eusebio Francisco Kino begins his missionary work in present-day Arizona.

1682
The first Texas mission is founded, in Corpus Christi.

1718
The Texas mission known as the Alamo is founded.

1769
Junípero Serra founds San Diego de Alcalá, the first mission in California.

1821
Mexico overthrows Spanish rule and becomes an independent nation.

1833–1834
The Mexican government assumes control of the missions; the lands are sold to farmers and ranchers.

1846–1848
The United States goes to war with Mexico and takes over much of the American Southwest.

Reference

Spanish Colonies

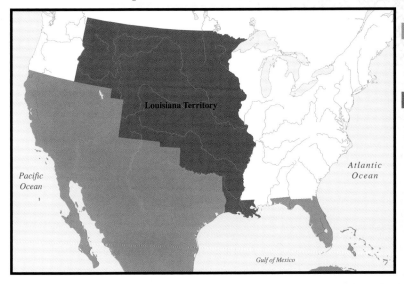

- North American land colonized by Spain
- Claimed by Spain (1760s-1800)

Spanish Missions in California

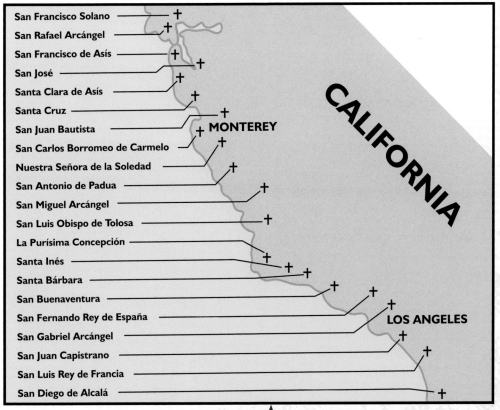

San Francisco Solano
San Rafael Arcángel
San Francisco de Asís
San José
Santa Clara de Asís
Santa Cruz
San Juan Bautista
San Carlos Borromeo de Carmelo
Nuestra Señora de la Soledad
San Antonio de Padua
San Miguel Arcángel
San Luis Obispo de Tolosa
La Purísima Concepción
Santa Inés
Santa Bárbara
San Buenaventura
San Fernando Rey de España
San Gabriel Arcángel
San Juan Capistrano
San Luis Rey de Francia
San Diego de Alcalá

MONTEREY
CALIFORNIA
LOS ANGELES

Websites to Visit

www.scholastic.com/teachers/article/spanish-missions-us-history

www.oldwestcountry.com/tmpl1.php?CID=ZKGNU

parks.ca.gov/?page_id=22722

Show What You Know

1. What was the purpose of a mission?

2. Describe the challenges priests faced.

3. How did missions change the lives of Native Americans?

4. Describe the hardships mission residents faced.

5. How are modern missions used today?

Glossary

adobe (ah-DOH-bee): sun-dried bricks made from sand, clay, and straw

Catholic (KATH-lihk): a member of a worldwide Christian religion that has been very prominent in Spain; the Spanish missionaries were Catholic

colonies (KOL-uh-neez): groups of people who settle in a distant land while remaining citizens of their original country; also the word for the place they settle

convert (KON-vurt): to convince or force someone to join a new religion; also, a person who leaves one religion to join another

drought (DROWT): a period when no rain falls, which goes on long enough to cause plants to die from lack of water

habit (HAB-it): the distinctive outfit of a priest or other religious person

hostile (HOS-tul): feeling or showing ill will

irrigation (IR-uh-GAY-shun): a man-made system of ditches and channels for bringing water to fields

natives (NAY-tihvz): born in a particular place or country

rituals (RITCH-u-uhlz): formal customs, usually religious, that are performed the same way year after year

Index